What's A Zombie To Do,
When His House Is Split In 2?

Written and Illustrated
By

Edward Kent

ISBN 13 - 978-1475263107
ISBN 10 -1475263104
LCCN:2012907715

This book is dedicated to my beautiful and supportive wife, partner, and best friend, Dannielle.

My three little zombies: Cordelia, Keifer and Brody.

A special thank you to Mrs. Wendy Gloss, principal at Windom Elementary in Orchard Park, NY, for all of her support and assistance, as well as the invaluable insights from her faculty and staff.

Zombie Ed and his little sister Jane,

MUDBERRY LN

live in a house on Mudberry Lane.

They have a dog named Spot, and a bony little fish.

But having Mom and Dad be happy is what they really wish.

Most of the time, usually late at night,

Ed and Jane have to listen to them yell and fight.

Once upon a time, they used to laugh and sing,

But now they just look sad, and that's a truly awful thing.

One day, Mom and Dad told them about the scary word "Divorce."

Both Ed and Jane thought, "What could possibly be worse?"

"We'll never see Dad, and we'll have to move away from our friends!"

"We'll lose all our stuff, so is THIS how it ends?"

"No more birthday parties, and no more holiday dinners!"

"It's not fair to us, so we're definitely not the winners!"

Mom and Dad could see that they were both upset, and very, very mad.

They tried hard to reassure them it wouldn't be so very bad.

"You'll have two rooms to sleep in, one here and one there,

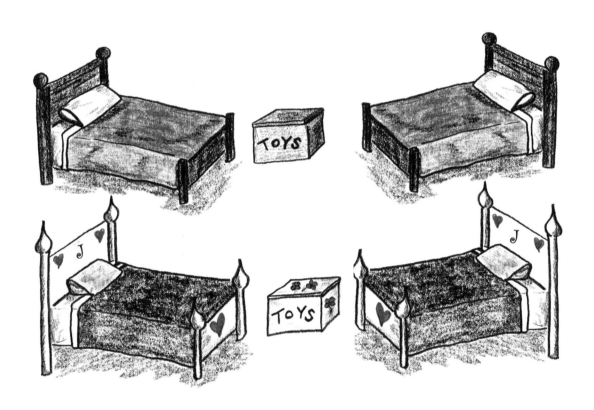

With lots of toys in each one, and plenty of new clothes to wear!"

Ed and Jane both knew that it wasn't new stuff that would make things okay,

But rather, for Mom and Dad to be friends again, and for Dad to stay.

Dad and Mom could see that their words were not helping much,

So they both decided to try a gentler touch.

"The problem is not with the two of you, so please try to see,

We love you both very much, and it's between Daddy and me."

Mom and Dad explained that because they couldn't get along,

Trying to live in the same house together wouldn't be right, it would be wrong.

They had talked and tried to make things all better,

But even though they worked real hard, it didn't seem to matter.

Ed and Jane were most important, you can forget all the rest.

Mom and Dad would be happy apart, so it would be for the best.

Ed knew deep down, that they were probably right.

And he and Jane both knew they hated to hear them fight.

Mom stayed in the house, and Dad moved downtown.

Ed was happy that he could stay at his school, because leaving would have been a letdown.

Dad's place was actually pretty cool.

It had a gym, a game room, and an awesome swimming pool!

Ed and Jane would go every weekend, and most holidays too,

Two Christmases, two Halloweens, and two trips to the zoo!

Mom ended up marrying a non-zombie named Jim,

who also had a little boy, and Ed enjoyed playing with him.

Dad married a teacher, and her name was Pam,

She has two little girls, so Jane's as happy as I am!

Don't get me wrong, I miss Mom and Dad being together, and in the same house everyday.

Both there morning, noon, and night, and watching us play.

Sometimes moms and dads stop loving each other and are happier apart and with someone new.

But always remember, no matter what, that it will NEVER mean they have stopped loving YOU!

Do You Remember?

1. What street did Jane and Ed live on?

2. What two pets did they have?

3. What was the scary word that Mom and Dad talked about?

4. What were Ed and Jane worried about?

5. What did Mom and Dad say was most important to them?

6. Why was it better that Mom and Dad live apart?

About the Author

Edward Kent lives in the quiet town of West Seneca, New York, located 15 minutes from downtown Buffalo, with his wife Dannielle, and their three children: Cordelia, Keifer, and Brody.

He grew up in a small town off Lake Ontario, and after high school, attended Niagara University where he received a BA, majoring in Theatre.

After receiving his Masters in Education, he taught second grade in Virginia Beach, Virginia for two years before relocating back to Western New York.

Time was spent teaching middle school, as well as working as a trainer for a major dialysis company, before beginning his new career as an author.

The author is a member of the Society of Children's Book Writers & Illustrators.

Visit the author at www.ZombieEdFun.com and http://ekent.blogspot.com/

Look for these other Zombie Ed titles:

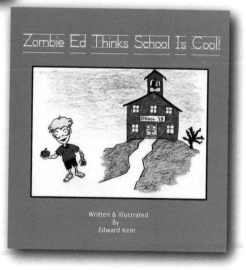

All titles available through the author's website at http://e-kent.blogspot.com/